The Hypersonic Duck

and Other Stories

Eltigani Ahmed

Contents

The Hypersonic Duck 1

Activity 1: Comprehension 11
Activity 2: Application 11
Activity 3: Lessons Learnt 12
Activity 4: New Words 12

Balena the Sinking Whale 13

Activity 1: Comprehension 23
Activity 2: Application 23
Activity 3: Lessons Learnt 24
Activity 4: New Words 24

The Indomitable Weasel 25

Activity 1: Comprehension 34
Activity 2: Application 34
Activity 3: Lessons Learnt 35
Activity 4: New Words 35

Nyika's Incredible Transformation 37

Activity 1: Comprehension 48
Activity 2: Application 48
Activity 3: Lessons Learnt 49
Activity 4: New Words 49

Treasures in the Cabin 51

Activity 1: Comprehension 60
Activity 2: Application 60
Activity 3: Lessons Learnt 61
Activity 4: New Words 61

The Hypersonic Duck

Story Background:

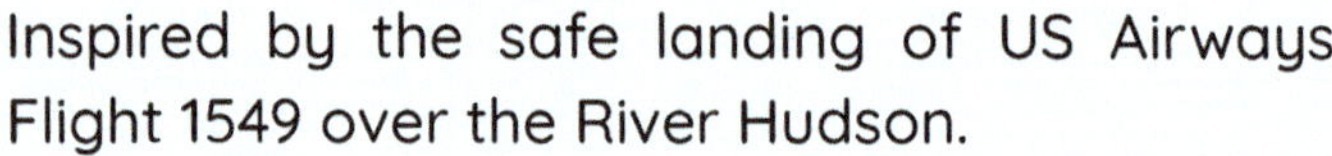

Inspired by the safe landing of US Airways Flight 1549 over the River Hudson.

Competences:

Practise, Focus, Determination

Social Values:

Generosity, Hard Work, Courage, Discipline

Summary:

Quacky lives in Avaria, a magnificent land with many trees and a home to many birds. Quacky is a super-ordinary duck who displayed unique skills such as high speed, stunts, and somersaults in the air that many of his friends admired. Quacky was not born with these skills. He acquired them through hard work and practise, after encouragement from his mother that he could do anything he put his mind to. Quacky manoeuvred a very dangerous whirlwind that many of his friends feared to attempt. Quacky was not mean; he freely shared his ideas and the secrets of his skills with his friends. Quacky's practise and preparation enabled him to face any unforeseen danger with calmness, intelligence and quick thinking.

The Hypersonic Duck

In the breathtaking land known as Avaria, where the bushy trees were home to many birds, there lived a little duck named Quacky. He was not an ordinary duck. Many of his friends referred to Quacky as a hypersonic duck! He zoomed through the skies faster than any other bird in Avaria.

His friends always admired Quacky's high speed, stunts and somersaults in the air. However, Quacky was not born that way. As a young duck, he had always admired the older birds and their amazing talents as they flew in the skies.

They made it look like it was so easy! He often wondered how he could improve his flying skills. He was determined to become the best among the birds that flew.

All Quacky could do, however, was waddle on the ground every day while wishing for a different kind of life.

"Quack! Quack!" he said as he flapped his wings and went about feeling sorry for himself.

One day, he decided that he would change his situation. He talked to his mother about his desire to be the best and fastest bird in the skies.

"You can do anything you put your mind to do, Quacky. Just work hard. If you want to succeed, you have to practise and prepare for it, every single day," she said.

Quacky promised himself that he would stop feeling sorry for himself. He would become self-disciplined and practise every day until he achieved success.

He remembered his mother's words; 'If you want to succeed, you have to practise and prepare for it, every single day.' Those words never left his mind. He practised taking off, flapping his wings and landing back on the ground. He fell and tumbled down many times as he practised.

A few of his friends even laughed at him when they saw his clumsy flying attempts. He ignored them and woke up every day to practise. He also read many books on how to become better at flying, ensuring that he applied everything he learnt.

After a while, Quacky succeeded and soared high in the skies. It was easy for him to fly past many of the birds in the air. He was excited that his dreams were finally coming to pass.

One sunny morning, as Quacky soared above the shimmering River Naisha, he spotted a group of his friends. They were training and practising their flying skills with the Flying School of Avaria. Quacky was excited to join them.

However, just as he was gliding along, a flock of mischievous geese flew by. They interrupted and disrupted the session with their loud noise, which caused chaos in the skies. They were all caught by surprise and had to dodge the attacking birds so as not to be harmed.

At the same time, a mighty whirlwind swept through the skies, which made all the birds spiral out of control! Quacky realised he had to think fast about what he needed to do. He remembered that in one of the books, he had read about Captain Featherwing who had dealt with a similar situation.

Drawing inspiration from the story, Quacky calmed his flapping wings and focused on steadying his flight. He remembered the importance of staying calm in the face of difficulty.

He also reminded himself of his mother's words, 'If you want to succeed, you must practise and prepare for it every day.' He had been preparing himself and practising for long hours each day. Now his hard work would pay off.

With his quick wit, Quacky managed to break free from the whirlwind, though he was now hurtling towards River Naisha at an alarming speed. At that moment, Quacky remembered something else from the story he had read. River Naisha was the same place Captain Featherwing had performed a spectacular landing years ago when he had to crash-land after encountering a whirlwind.

Quacky gathered all his courage and stabilised his hypersonic flight into a controlled drop as he approached the river. With determination and skill, he managed to pull off a perfect landing, splashing gracefully onto the water and coming to a gentle stop.

Quacky's friends who were watching everything that had happened cheered him on. They quacked and sang. Others cooed and chirped, while some hooted, screeched and flapped their wings in delight.

All were amazed at Quacky's daring feat! Learners from the Flying School of Avaria gathered around Quacky, eager to learn from his experience.

Quacky was happy to share the lessons he had learnt about the importance of continuous practise and preparation. This ensured that any unforeseen danger was met with calmness, as well as intelligence and quick thinking. He had mastered these valuable lessons from his numerous hours of working hard to become better.

Quacky became a celebrity and continued working with the younger birds, training them to become the best they could be as they flew in the skies. He even established a school to train younger birds how to perform and perfect their acrobatic moves. He collaborated with the Flying School of Avaria, which trained the birds how to improve on their flying skills.

Together, they had greater accomplishments. All the birds learnt the importance of ensuring they always practised and prepared, so they would be ready to face whatever came their way.

Activity 1 — Comprehension

1. What made Quacky different from other birds in Avaria?

2. What are some of the things Quacky did to become good at flying?

3. What were Quacky and his friends doing when they encountered trouble in the skies?

4. What did Quacky remember that helped him to navigate the challenge he encountered?

5. What were the main lessons that Quacky learnt from his experience, and shared with other learners from the Flying School of Avaria?

Activity 2 — Application

The following activity will require extended time for you to achieve and see the results.

What have you been struggling to work on lately, but are not getting the results you want? Write it down. Take some time to practise and prepare as many times as you can, until you become better at it. Then come back and write down your results. Share the news with your friends.

What have you learnt from this story?

Check your dictionary or search on the internet with the help of your teacher or parent, and write down the meaning of the following new words. The first two have been done for you.

1. Celebrity – one who is famous or well known.

2. Dodge – to move suddenly from side to side or to and fro, especially to avoid being hit by something, like an object.

3. Feat - ____

4. Hurtle - ____

5. Hypersonic - _______________________________________

6. Mischievous - ______________________________________

7. Self-discipline - ____________________________________

8. Shimmer - ____

9. Waddle - ____

10. Wit - ____

Balena
the
Sinking Whale

Story Background:
Inspired by the Titanic

Competences:
Creativity, Problem-Solving, Citizenship

Social Values:
Kindness, Bravery, Selflessness, Friendship

Summary:

Balena was an enormous whale with a sleek, black and white body that glistened under the sun. Balena lived in the vast expanse of the Indian Ocean. He lived in the best part of the ocean, a beautiful and colourful spot known as Aqua Heaven. Balena was brave and gentle. The long-awaited oceanic gala was finally organised, and the animals looked forward to it. Balena offered to ferry the animals to the gala. However, he had to fight a floating iceberg first. He had to fight for his own life. The sea creatures survived to tell the story of the selfless Balena.

Balena
the
Sinking Whale

Once upon a time, in the vast expanse of the Indian Ocean, there was a magnificent whale named Balena. Balena was unlike any other whale. He was enormous, with a sleek, black and white body that glistened under the sun. His heart was full of kindness, and he was also known to have a sense of adventure. This made him the most loved and famous whale in the ocean.

Balena lived in a kingdom where everyone admired him for his bravery and gentle nature. His home was a magical place called Aqua Haven. It was a paradise beneath the waves, filled with colourful corals, and playful fish and dolphins.

One day, a grand celebration, the great ocean gala, was planned in Aqua Haven. Invitations were sent to creatures from all corners of the ocean to come and celebrate their unity and friendship. Being the beloved whale, Balena was chosen to ferry the guests from their various habitats to the gala on his back.

Excitement echoed through the waves among the creatures in the ocean as the gala drew near. On the day of the celebration, Balena, adorned with sparkling seashells and colourful seaweed, eagerly awaited the arrival of his guests.

The sea turtles, the octopuses, and even the dolphins, everyone hopped onto Balena's back, ready for the grand adventure. Balena glided through the waves while his guests chatted excitedly as they enjoyed the ride.

They all joined in the celebration on arrival. Each guest mingled with creatures they had not seen for a while, since their last gala. As the event kicked off, however, an unexpected thing happened. An iceberg which had broken off from the frozen north floated into the warm waters.

Balena was so engrossed in entertaining the guests that he did not notice the looming danger until it was too late. The iceberg floated closer and closer to Aqua Haven. In spite of Balena's efforts to steer it away, he realised that a collision was imminent.

The iceberg struck Balena's side with a thunderous force. He felt the pain of the impact go through his entire body. He should have thought of saving himself, but instead, he began prompting all the guests to evacuate Aqua Haven. He felt his fins go numb and knew that he had been severely hurt.

The gala became chaotic as the guests tried to save Balena, but he was too big for them. With his strength growing weaker, but his heart full of courage, Balena urged all his guests to swim to safety. He realised that he was getting faint and losing consciousness as he started to sink.

Despite his best efforts to stay afloat, Balena descended deeper and deeper into the ocean. His massive body gradually disappeared into the dark bottom of the ocean. The creatures watched in shock and sadness as their beloved friend, the heroic whale, descended into the depths of the ocean.

After a while, they could no longer see Balena, however much they kept hoping he would resurface. They were all deeply saddened that they were unable to save him.

But wait! The spirit of Balena lived on. His selflessness had touched the hearts of all the creatures in the ocean. He had clearly demonstrated that he was more concerned with the needs and safety of other creatures than himself. He was their hero.

They vowed to honour his memory by always selflessly helping each other in times of need, and cherishing the gift of friendship at all times.

From that day on, the tale of Balena the sinking whale echoed through the oceans. The older creatures taught the younger ones the importance of being selfless in their service to others and remaining united as a community.

Every year after that, on the night of the great ocean gala, the sea creatures would gather to share stories of Balena, ensuring that his legacy lived on forever.

 Activity **1** **Comprehension**

1. Who was the main character in the story and what made him unique?

2. What was the special event happening in Aqua Haven, and why was it important?

3. What unexpected danger approached during the great ocean gala?

4. What did Balena do when the iceberg struck him?

5. What did the other creatures do to honour his memory?

 Activity **2** **Application**

Balena thought about his friends and made sure that he saved their lives when there was danger. Share with your classmates or family some acts of selflessness you did and the impact these deeds had on others.

Activity **3**   **Lessons Learnt**

What have you learnt from this story?

Activity **4**   **New Words**

Check your dictionary or search on the internet with the help of your teacher or parent, and write down the meaning of the following new words. The first two have been done for you.

1. Collision - a violent and forceful coming together of two or more objects.

2. Engross - to absorb or consume all of one's attention, time or interest.

3. Evacuate - ____

4. Expanse - ____

5. Gala - ____

6. Glisten - ____

7. Iceberg - ____

8. Imminent - ____

9. Legacy - ____

10. Sleek - ____

The Indomitable Weasel

Story Background:

Inspired by honey badger's bravery and resilience

Competences:

Efficiency,
Determination,
Learning

Social Values:

Self-Efficacy,
Determination,
Courage

Summary:

Whisker is a curious and spirited weasel living in Kenya's Aberdare Ranges. Whisker is small but courageous. One breezy morning, he visited the honey badger in his den. The honey badger was known all over the forest for his courage and resilience. Whisker learnt from the honey badger that being resilient was not dependent on the size of his body but the belief in his mind and the conviction in his heart. He realised that he was capable of doing anything he desired if he believed in himself and refused to give up.

The Indomitable Weasel

A curious and spirited weasel named Whisker lived in a lavish forest in the Aberdare Ranges. Whisker was not the largest or strongest animal in the forest. What he lacked in size, however, he made up for with courage and determination.

Whisker was known as 'the indomitable weasel' because of his fearless nature. He loved exploring every nook and cranny of the forest. He boldly climbed the highest trees, just for fun. He also enjoyed making his way into the burrows of the tiniest creatures in the forest.

Whisker was not afraid of encountering danger. He courageously confronted and tackled any risks that lurked within the forest. His adventures were well known and many animals admired his fearlessness.

One sunny day, a group of animals gathered near the stream. They quenched their thirst as they chatted about the honey badger, who was the fiercest and most resilient creature in the forest. They whispered tales of his legendary battles and how he outwitted even the largest predators.

Whisker's ears perked up as he listened intently to the conversation.

"I heard that he fought off two young lions last week, imagine that!" the hare exclaimed.

"My goodness! What a bold fellow! Not too long ago, he survived a poisonous bite from the cobra because of his thick skin. I certainly would not want to cross his path!" the porcupine chipped in.

"I wonder if I could be as resilient and brave as the honey badger," Whisker thought to himself as the conversation among the animals went on.

Determined to learn and increase his knowledge on being more resilient, Whisker set off on a quest to meet the honey badger.

Along the way, he found a fox, a bear and an owl gathered under a tree. He overheard their conversation as they discussed the honey badger, and how many challenges he had survived. These stories of resilience made Whisker even more eager to find the honey badger.

After several days of his journey, Whisker finally got to the honey badger's den. The honey badger stared at Whisker with fearless eyes and regarded him with curiosity.

"I have heard many tales of your incredible resilience," Whisker said, trying to match the honey badger's steady gaze. "I want to learn from you."

The honey badger chuckled. "Resilience and bravery are not about how big or small you are, little weasel," he said. "It is about having the heart of a warrior, no matter how small you are."

Impressed by Whisker's determination, the honey badger agreed to teach him a few life lessons on resilience.

"First, you must understand that your resilience is all in the mind, not necessarily in your size. You can withstand any challenge that comes your way. You can regain your balance and keep your foes away. Never forget that!" the honey badger started off.

Whisker nodded his head
and made a mental note to
always remember that.

"Next, keep gathering information from your environment. Information will enhance your ability to make quick decisions and solve problems swiftly. This will always come in handy, whatever situation you find yourself in. I have survived in different habitats, including arid regions, wet places and under water. This is because I learn and adapt quickly to my environment."

"Third, do not waste all your energy on one difficult situation because a more challenging one could come up soon. You should always keep an eye on the unforeseen."

"In addition, I urge you to remain confident in your capabilities. Everything you need to be resilient and remain confident is right inside you. You see, my tough skin enables me to survive bites from my enemies. I also have immunity from the venom of scorpions or snakes that could harm me. You need to look at your natural, inborn abilities. You will realise that you have exactly what it takes to be resilient!" the honey badger said.

Whisker was amazed at this detailed explanation. He was delighted that the honey badger was so generous with the information.

As the two spent more time together, Whisker realised that being resilient was not just about facing off the big foes of the jungle. It was about believing in oneself and never giving up, no matter the odds.

With new-found confidence, Whisker thanked the honey badger, bid him farewell and started his journey home. He might have been small, but now felt in his heart that he was truly indomitable.

The lessons he had learnt on resilience gave him greater boldness to face challenges.

From that day, Whisker's adventures became even more legendary. He inspired other animals with his tales of resilience and bravery. He showed them that the confidence in their hearts and their belief in themselves mattered more than the size of their bodies.

He continued roaming the forest, fearlessly exploring and teaching others the true meaning of resilience.

Activity 1 — Comprehension

1. Why was Whisker referred to as 'the indomitable weasel'?

2. Why did Whisker embark on a quest to meet the honey badger?

3. What made Whisker even more eager to meet the honey badger as he was on his way?

4. What did Whisker learn from the honey badger during their time together?

5. How did Whisker inspire other animals in the forest when he returned from his journey?

Activity 2 — Application

Get a pen and a book or a piece of paper. Write down some of your strengths, or what you believe you are good at. You can also ask your parents, siblings, teachers or friends what they think you are good at. Then list how the qualities you have identified can help you remain resilient when faced with difficult situations. Share what you have written with your parents, teachers and friends.

Activity 3 Lessons Learnt

What have you learnt from this story?

Activity 4 New Words

Check your dictionary or search on the internet with the help of your teacher or parent, and write down the meaning of the following new words. The first two have been done for you.

1. Chuckle - to laugh inwardly or quietly.

2. Immunity - the quality or state of being resistant to a disease.

3. Indomitable -

4. Lavish -

5. Legendary -

6. Lurk -

7. Perk -

8. Quench -

9. Quest -

10. Spirited -

Nyika's
Incredible
Transformation

Story Background:

The story aims to promote the protection of the environment and biodiversity

Competences:

Communication, Problem-Solving, Citizenship

Social Values:

Resilience, Patriotism, Hard Work, Courage

Summary:

Frasha is a joyful butterfly who lived in a one-time heavenly land called Nyika. Frasha always spread the cheer with her two friends, Benny, the bee, and Lila, the ladybird, who liked to gather on a shrub with beautiful flowers and chat for hours. However, the land had become dry, causing many plants and shrubs to die. This pushed Frasha to charge her friends to join her in restoring their formerly beautiful land. Everyone had a role to play. They watered the plants, and the bees worked hard to pollinate the flowers. Their efforts paid off as they began to see the transformation in their land.

Nyika's Incredible Transformation

Far, far away, in the deserted and parched land known as Nyika, there once lived a butterfly whose name was Frasha. She was a joyful little creature who loved to spread cheer wherever she went. Her friends, Benny the bee and Lila the ladybird, were always looking out for her company. She was sure to light up the mood whenever she showed up. They loved to gather in their favourite spot, on a shrub with beautiful flowers, where they would chat for hours.

Over time, however, there was little to light up the mood in their environment. The land had become dry and many of the plants that sustained them had begun to wither. The cracked land was thirsty for rain.

The withering plants had seen better days, and the heat from the sun seemed to get hotter and hotter by the day. Indeed, quite a number of animals had migrated elsewhere to go and look for better pastures.

Frasha was particularly discouraged about the state of things. She was dismayed by what she saw as she looked around her. She called her two friends as she wanted to share her concerns with them.

"**Bzzzz! Bzzzz!** Hello Frasha, why do you look so sad today? It is unlike you to look gloomy," Benny the Bee started off.

"Yes, Frasha. What is the matter?" Lila the ladybird asked.

Frasha was quiet for a moment, as she remembered a story that her grandmother had told her when she was young. She recalled her grandmother saying that the animals at the time had also faced similar circumstances.

The land had been dry and the rains had taken a long time before they fell. However, the animals had come together and discussed how they would bring solutions to the challenge they faced.

They had worked together to make their environment the kind of home they would enjoy living in. Frasha's grandmother talked about how beautiful the land eventually became, after the collective effort from all the animals.

Once again, the insects and animals thrived, the rains fell in the right season, and all the animals had sufficient food to eat. It seemed that along the way, the animals had abandoned their roles and the consequences were now evident.

"Well, look around you. Aren't you concerned about the deplorable state of our surroundings? I wonder what happened to the once beautiful place my grandmother told me about. She told me that all the animals had worked together to conserve their environment, but we seem to have forgotten all about that," Frasha said.

She went on to narrate her grandmother's story, and told her friends that they had to do something, and fast! The three friends agreed to involve other animals and insects, as they embarked on the journey of environmental conservation. Thankfully, the other animals agreed to cooperate and they got to work. They all longed to see their home restored to its former beauty.

Everyone had a role to play. The ants, the beetles and the birds assisted with seed dispersal. They scattered the seeds of different plants far and wide so that there would be more vegetation. The elephants used their trunks to carry water and sprinkle it on the plants.

The bees and butterflies worked hard to pollinate the few flowers they could find. They transferred the pollen from one flower to the next so the plants could reproduce. All the animals met regularly to learn how else they could preserve their environment, and to give updates of what they had been doing.

The work was tiring because some of the insects could only transport one seed at a time. The bees and butterflies sometimes could not find enough flowers to pollinate. The few flowers they found were far apart and the distances they had to fly were long. They often got discouraged when they came to some flowers and found that they had already withered.

A few birds got hungry along the way and swallowed the seeds before they could get to their destination to plant them. Some also complained about how the heat from the blazing sun was wearing them down. There were many things that came up to demoralise the animals. However, they refused to quit, and encouraged each other to keep going.

After some time, the rains eventually fell. The animals waited with bated breath to see what would become of their efforts. Gradually, the seeds sprouted, the flowers bloomed and blossomed, and the land became green again. It took time, but the animals began to realise that their efforts had paid off. They gathered to celebrate the transformation of the land.

Frasha, Benny and Lila were delighted that they had taken the first step, and that they had involved the other animals.

"We shall continue to educate all the creatures around us about environmental conservation. We all have a part to play in preserving our habitat!" Frasha said.

Everyone agreed with her and they all made a decision never to let their environment deteriorate again. They would do their best to ensure that it continued to flourish and thrive.

 Activity **1** **Comprehension**

1. What was unique about Frasha?

2. Why did Frasha get concerned as she looked around her?

3. What story had Frasha's grandmother told her about the place where they lived?

4. Explain some of the challenges that the animals encountered as they worked towards conserving their environment.

5. How was Nyika transformed after all the hard work from the animals?

 Activity **2** **Application**

Make a list of the things human beings do to destroy the environment. Then come up with some of the actions that you and your classmates or friends will take to conserve your environment. Do at least one thing on your list to conserve the environment during your school term and one thing during your holidays.

Activity 3 — Lessons Learnt

What have you learnt from this story?

Activity 4 — New Words

Check your dictionary or search on the internet with the help of your teacher or parent, and write down the meaning of the following new words. The first two have been done for you.

1. Bated breath – to eagerly anticipate something.

2. Bloom - to produce flowers.

3. Consequences - ________________________

4. Deplorable - ________________________

5. Dismay - ________________________

6. Environmental conservation - ________________________

7. Migrate - ________________________

8. Parched - ________________________

9. Pollinate - ________________________

10. Wither - ________________________

Treasures in the Cabin

Story Background:

The story aims to promote kindness and selflessness

Competences:

Communication, Citizenship, Integrity

Social Values:

Benevolence, Exploration, Love

Summary:

Charity was an adventurous young girl who loved exploring the forest near her hometown of Ubuntu. She was also incredibly talented and could spot beauty in the simplest things around her. It started raining during one of her adventures in the forest, and Charity took shelter in an old cabin. She discovered a dusty, handwritten book of a wealthy traveller, along with his great wealth, hidden in the cabin. The traveller had requested the person who would find the book to be generous and share his wealth with others. Being an honest girl, Charity informed her parents about her discovery, and ultimately, the entire village benefited from the treasure.

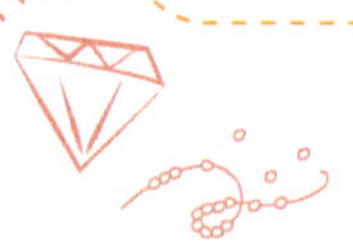

Treasures in the Cabin

In the bustling town of Ubuntu, there was a young girl named Charity who loved exploring the forest near her home. Charity was ten years old and had an incredible talent for spotting beauty in the simplest of things. One stormy afternoon, a sudden downpour surprised her as she ventured into the woods. Seeking shelter, she stumbled upon an old, abandoned cabin deep in the forest. She decided to step inside and wait for the rain to stop.

The cabin was filled with dusty books and trinkets. As she looked around, her eyes fell upon a weathered book tucked away in a corner. She could not hold herself back, so she went over and opened it. Charity discovered that it contained a handwritten story of a wealthy traveller who had faced numerous challenges but found purpose through each trial.

The traveller had lived in the cabin during his final days. They were mostly spent writing about his journeys across numerous places, where he had met many people and acquired a lot of wealth. He shared the wealth of wisdom he had acquired in his story. Along with it, he gave details of the riches he had accumulated.

Towards the end of the book, the traveller had hoped that a kind soul would find it, and be generous enough to help other people with the treasures he had left behind. In closing, the traveller had ended his book with the following words:

'Never get tired of doing little things for others, sometimes those little things occupy the biggest parts of their hearts.'

Charity thought about how lucky she was to have stumbled upon the cabin and found the book. She had the traveller's entire wealth at her disposal and she could do with it whatever she wanted. She decided to run back home and tell her parents what she had found. Charity was eager to share the new-found wealth with her entire community.

When the rain stopped, she ran back home and shared the news with her parents. They were happy about her honesty and informed the village chief about it. Her friend Grabby, however, mocked her when she found out about Charity's discovery.

"How could you? Why did you have to share such a secret with anyone? You could have kept it to yourself and only told me! We would have been rich forever, and never have needed to share the riches with anybody else!" she lamented bitterly.

Charity felt discouraged by Grabby's words, but knew deep down in her heart, that she had done the right thing.

In the meantime, the village chief asked a few young men to begin digging for the treasure that the traveller had buried, as they followed the directions in the book. They discovered large amounts of gold, silver and other precious stones buried in treasure chests. It took them several days to finally unearth it all.

The villagers thanked Charity for being such a generous little girl, and her honesty was rewarded. Her family was given a large portion of the treasure. Charity was also made part of the team that would oversee how the rest of the treasure would be used, especially to help other village children like her.

The wise village chief decided he would respect the wishes of the wealthy traveller and follow the example set by Charity. Her family may not have had much, but Charity had chosen not to keep the treasure to herself. She shared it with the community. Charity's mother told her it was an act of philanthropy, since she had been so generous in sharing what she had with others.

The chief set up many projects in the village that grew the wealth of the community. The sick were taken care of, the orphans were provided for, and the needy were assisted with what they required. The villagers found innovative ways to assist others. The people thrived and grew very rich over time.

Charity's philanthropic example influenced the entire community. They became generous in giving their time and resources to each other. Everyone who was assisted was encouraged to do the same for ten others. This created a ripple effect of generosity and goodwill.

The neighbouring villages caught on and flourished in their businesses as they followed this example. Charity's story was added to the annals of the traveller's book, as a continuation of the narrative. Her name and fame were included and highly esteemed in every tale that was ever told about the treasures hidden in the wealthy traveller's cabin.

Treasures
in the
Cabin

Activity 1 — Comprehension

1. What was special about Charity?

2. What unique item did Charity find in the old cabin?

3. What quote did the wealthy traveller end his story with?

4. Why was Grabby, Charity's friend, angry with her?

5. How did the entire community benefit from Charity's act of being philanthropic?

Activity 2 — Application

The following activity will require extended time for you to achieve and see the results.

What are some of the ways you have followed Charity's example by being philanthropic to others around you? With help from your teachers or parents, plan an activity that will allow you to show genuine philanthropy to needy people around you.

Activity 3 — Lessons Learnt

What have you learnt from this story?

Activity 4 — New Words

Check your dictionary or search on the internet with the help of your teacher or parent, and write down the meaning of the following new words. The first two have been done for you.

1. Annals - a record of events or historical records.

2. Bustling – used to refer to a place that is full of activity.

3. Esteem - _______________________________________

4. Innovative - _______________________________________

5. Lament - _______________________________________

6. Philanthropy - _______________________________________

7. Ripple effect - _______________________________________

8. Trinkets - _______________________________________

9. Unearth - _______________________________________

10. Venture - _______________________________________

Acknowledgements

I am enormously grateful to the remarkable team who worked tirelessly to bring this book to life.

I thank, in particular, Truphena Njiru, who coordinated the entire project with unmatched professionalism. The beauty of this book will bear lasting witness to her selfless dedication.

I thank Patricia Businge for executing a complex yet intriguingly captivating interior layout.

I thank Tewis Kimingi for elegantly creating an artistic masterpiece of the front and back covers.

I thank Davis Bamwine and Eric Muchira for skillfully executing the illustrations and transforming the text into a visually engaging experience.

I thank Sylvance Mboha for his insightful critiques and thought-sharing.

I thank Tamador for her love and support.

I thank Aiman, Muhannad, Areej, Mohamed, and Arwa (or the team Amama) for sharing their thoughts on the stories.

I thank every person who contributed to this book and whose name I might have inadvertently omitted. Their names shall be preserved in the readers' memories.